THE PUNISHMENTS MUST BE A SCHOOL

THE
PUNISHMENTS
MUST BE A SCHOOL

Emily August

THE WORD WORKS
WASHINGTON, D.C.

Cover Design: Susan Pearce Design
Cover Art: Shawna Gilmore, "A Boar and Bear Battle in the Big Woods"

Library of Congress Control Number: 2023944155
International Standard Book Number: 978-1-944585-64-8

Acknowledgments

Thank you to the editors and readers of the publications in which these poems first appeared, sometimes in different versions or with different titles:

Callaloo: "The Oracle"
Cider Press Review: "Art History," "Lessons in Physics"
Cimarron Review: "Beyond the Frame"
Hayden's Ferry Review: "End of Days," "The Gloomy Festival of
    Punishment"
Midway Journal: "The Punishments Must Be a School"
Missouri Review (Poem of the Week): "Black-Eyed Susan"
Ninth Letter: "The Split Fig"
Paradigm: "The Magician, Reversed"
Quarterly West: "Almost Without Touching the Body," "Prayer for
    the Withheld Interior"
Rove: "The Lost"
Southern Humanities Review: "The Healer"

Thank you to Nancy White and The Word Works for believing in this book and bringing it into the world as a tangible artifact.

Thank you to the literary kinfolk who graciously evaluated these poems throughout the years. Your guidance helped me incise, excise, dissect, and suture these poems into their thriving selves, and our zany creative adventures have kept the spirit of poetry beating in my heart. I extend particular gratitude to Elizabeth Barnett, Lisa Dordal, Keegan Cook Finberg, Deborah Keenan, Cynthia Arrieu-King, my dear University of Minnesota cohort, and the many more teachers, mentors, and colleagues who shaped this book in myriad ways.

Thank you to the people whose friendship and support uplifted me during the long, lean years of this book's journey, including Faith Barter, Nicole Collins-Kwong, Michelle Livingston, Nathan Long, and Corynn Stoltenberg, and the many more friends and loved ones who sustained me, including my many "anonymous" recovery soulmates. Robin Rozanski, I think you would've liked this book, and I picture you reading it on a window seat in your gothic Victorian mansion in the sky.

Thank you to my mother, Joan—my best friend, my north star, and a wise and gifted healer. How lucky I am to know you and be guided by you.

Contents

I. The Organs of Generation

II. The Articulations

III. Embryology

IV. Osteology

V. The Blood-Vascular System

VI. The Lymphatics

VII. The Organs of Special Sense

"The punishments must be a school; an ever-open book. Children should be allowed to come to the places where the penalty is carried out."

—Michel Foucault, *Discipline and Punish*

"This feels like school, somehow. Except at school they didn't execute you at the end. Unless you went to a really fucking tough school."

—Martin McDonagh, *The Pillowman*

I.

The Organs of Generation

"They project into the spaces. They are remarkable
for their tortuous course in the substance of the organ."

—Henry Gray
Anatomy, Descriptive and Surgical (1858)

The Healer

Nothing existed. Then, the sea. Dreaming,
it drew wooden ships into being. Then flesh
to maneuver them. Above the fathoms,

muscled in mist, we amassed a cargo
of artifacts. Prized shell
of the lightning whelk. A jade urn

collecting our ashes. Cinnamon quills
and saffron, suspended from twine. Shy thrust
of the jonquil, tended by deckhands, nurtured

in brine. And the enjambment
of the black nudes, organized
in the chambers below

by the logic of anguish. Unlike us,
they could not learn
from punishment.

The pale boy at the Arctic Circle
ran so fast toward the boat
his shoelace came untied. His palms

collected sweat, refusing
his only possessions:
glass jars of fish the cobblestones cut open.

We floated into the noiseless, white
distance. Above, we sickened. Below, the cargo
weakened, until the pale boy

calculated our losses and heaved them
over the ship's edge. Nobody asked
for forgiveness. During a storm, the ship split

to spill us. Our clothes were so tattered
they couldn't uphold us above the sea; the sea
pulled us under its breaking white wave.

In the silence of the wreckage, hair hovered
above the heads of the drowned. Those who were left
converted the strands to thread

and sewed the skins of the dead into sails
to tie to the masts of our legs. The cold wind
carved us a path to an unfamiliar shore.

Though we have invaded the land, still,
we can't make a life here. The winter
tortures us each year, until we're consumed

by failure. We whip our children with switches
fashioned from the dead crops,
to help them understand

agriculture. In the wasted fields,
the pale boy breaks our bones
and starts our old wounds freshly bleeding,

in order to teach us
how to survive in this place,
and to teach himself healing.

The Oracle

I slipped my shackles and hid
at the pier. Shadows
became tactile there.
The stevedores spit
tentacles of tobacco and keened
for their missing freight: I had tipped
from the ship's rusted pocket,
unloading myself at midnight's bell. I fell
into a squid's hiss, his prophecy
curling blacker
against black waters. That ink,
I heard later, had spun
to embrace the hull,
spelling disaster. It could not be abraded
with salt.

That permanence followed me
everywhere. In the taverns
that bordered the shore,
I rubbed strong beer against my teeth,
but my tongue could not corrode
the sea's grit. I licked
brine from my palms
and tasted shades
of the oyster. In a clouded slip of glass,
I discovered my mouth
had also blackened.

Always, I would speak the black stain.

II.

The Articulations

"In the adult this suture is generally obliterated
and the bone forms one piece; traces of the obliterated
suture are, however, generally perceptible."

—Henry Gray
Anatomy, Descriptive and Surgical (1858)

The Warning Wood

We arrived on the land, and its emptiness
told us it belonged to us. We took

the first layer of the tree line
and milled it to build.

Outside the house, the crops
are silent now. The dead meadow

stretches from the porch
all the way to the wood.

Beyond the field, the pines creak
with language.

They form a flank
along the property's edge.

The canary enters the wood
and never returns.

The wolves bring us milk
that tastes of cardamom and fig.

They plunder the forest and carry us
rabbits and mice, which they scatter

just past the border. They warn us
there is no lesson in the carcass.

In the house, the smell of the fallen
can't reach us.

Like a sunflower's pollen, blood
coats the fields.

The canary enters the wood ahead of us,
and never returns.

Black-Eyed Susan

Grandfather sharpens
the kitchen knives at his whetstone.

The wounded haunt
the fields of switchgrass that smother

the farm. Choked in heather
up to its tarpaper,

the rotting shed at the property's edge
slowly dilapidates into the bed

of black-eyed Susan
planted long ago at its door.

Inside its walls, the tractor chains
grandfather inherited hang despondent,

clogged with the skins of the last generation
of crops. Grandfather labors

at the creek's water,
holding the heads of his children

under. Grandfather looms
over his children, instilling

the belt. Grandfather blinds
his children's eyes, seeking

the source of memory,
but he cannot erase himself

from the distance: the children bloom
into bruises of amber and green,

and they cultivate new blooms of blood
along their own children's cheeks.

Eventually, all the children are born with scars
that mimic the tremor of household stitches,

lining their tiny bodies like old ghosts
who sharpen knives in the kitchen.

Beyond the Frame

Mother darkens the bedroom doorway.
Her shadow damages the shapes
the room otherwise makes: the flowering spread

and bedside slippers assume sinister silhouettes.
The children crouch inside the closet,
leaving it open just a crack. They don't hold hands.

Outside, as a newborn moth panics
against the chain link fence, the children sense father
deeper in the hallway, escaping

the room's edge. He too casts a pall, shrouding
mother. He must be hulking
beside her, preparing his fists beyond the frame.

Mother, threatened and threatening,
it's hard to know who you're protecting.
Outside, the moth

must weigh the energy it will take
to free itself, and to mend
the injuries its wings incur. To survive,

it must believe in the cone of dust
that the light makes visible. Its life is so brief—
it could seem easier to stay caught there.

The Lost

In the pines, the siblings
tie their hands behind their backs

and scream. Tornados
hover the lakes—no place

to hide. Limbs are dredged
from the murk. The work

is a kind of murder.
The forest path is paved

by the pulver left over
after the facts have been rehearsed

down to grit. The lesson gets harder to learn
like this. Like beating

a corpse—that horse
can't run. You can know every story and, still,

the heart remains unsolved.
In the pines,

a humid echo clings to the needles.
The only evidence left of the bodies

after the bodies
have disappeared.

Pine Song

You laid me down in the woods,
in the Jersey woods, in the woods
of Pennsylvania. You laid me down without me
having to ask. The devil
unburdened inside me as I looked up
into the barrens, into the wet
October, atop the carpet
of needles. When you laid me down
and I bent my back, the devil came
without my asking; the devil
came from the woods
like a white machine.

The Descendants

We couldn't forgive ourselves
for becoming statuary. For inheriting

the bent posture of the cursed.
We couldn't expect the universe

to rewind itself, or the punishments
to be reversed. The rusted car on the lawn

was our only possession, waiting
to be repurposed. But it couldn't

be stripped of the moss
that clung to its frame.

We gathered each Easter
to rehearse the childhood occurrences,

when we were bent beneath the wounds
that tutored us. It was a ritual penance

to balance the silent year ahead,
when the memories couldn't be coerced

from their moist habitat
inside our mouths. When we cradled our guilt

because its fat made us
warm, protecting our joints.

When we coddled our shame, because it made us
human; because it felt like thirst.

Family Practice

From the moment we're born
our bodies are burdens.
Our mothers pass down

the cradle song,
willing the bough
to break. Our fathers pass down

the myth of Icarus, willing
our wings to unfasten.
We pass down the cookbooks

from matriarch to daughter—
generations and generations
of bourbon, tobacco, and sugar.

Ribboned in fat, we tender
toward the ghosts in the attic, hoping
to be inhabited.

We hoard the old sicknesses
as misers; cultivate
the cadaver's complaint.

We use the ghosts' hands
to build the property of our bodies
in their image.

Finally, organs fail us. Lesions leave us
lean. We crackle like a light bulb
burning out, then a wisp of steam.

Doctor, if you see us start
to revert back into skin,
withhold your medicine.

They Say Trauma

My grandfather was a long-haul trucker.
When he was gone it was passable, living
in squalor. When he was home, he battered his children
within an inch of torture.

When they grew up, each sibling
made themselves a promise.
They were so careful.

Only once, my mother
spanked me. I was already too old for it.
She called me to her lap,
and her knees cracked
as I draped over it.

I laughed as she swung. I taunted her
over and over. *It doesn't hurt*, I told her.
She wept the whole way through.
I glanced behind me as I left
the room. I saw her shoulders
bent in self-loathing.
Even at the age of ten, I understood
I'd broken her. We never spoke of it.

When my grandfather died, the family
gathered at his property:
a single-wide trailer
and a rotting shed. He'd settled
far north, at the state's most rural edge, hunkered
among a century's hoard
of useless and discarded objects:
rusted milk jugs, crusty overalls,
castoff parts from vintage engines,
containers and containers of batteries
leached of their acid.

I was the studious one, a little too smart
right out of the womb, so I got to pick
through his leftover books.
I found a moldy dictionary
buried under the stacks.

It's so seductive
to believe that this is the sum
of what he bequeathed me.

Instead, I often wonder if his legacy
is how I came to let a person
I was fucking beat me.

They say trauma
is returning, again
and again, to the moment of harm,
in an attempt to reclaim and revise it.

An impossible task—you were never present
to begin with.

They say trauma is remembered
in our cells; even passed
to our children.

Maybe I never
had a chance, then. Maybe his hands
were already hammering me
before I was born.

III.

Embryology

"The extreme complexity of the process
of development renders it at all times difficult
to describe intelligibly."

—Henry Gray
Anatomy, Descriptive and Surgical (1858)

Instruction

Once I was as wild
as a crab apple tree.
Then it was time for school.

The teacher clapped chalk
from her hands
and the white dust settled.

I couldn't cut
a folded piece of paper
into a snowflake—
after I spread the paper open,
I always wound up
with two separate halves.

At my little desk, I strained
to be a person. The desk
asked me to be smaller.

Instruction
should've made me fit,
but I haven't yet.

The Punishments Must Be a School

I was the child born hybrid
from the fissure—bursting

from the black rock of the earth
in a plume of white ash,

rendered from magnets, minerals,
and medicinal plants. If you bit me

hard enough to break skin, I would
poison you.

The other children poked me
with willow branches,

but they couldn't deliver
the hot copper from my veins.

I slept under snow,
hoping my body

would freeze and crack;
that my soul would steam upwards.

I only melted a circle around me
by morning.

I could never remember
my lessons, so when the teacher chose me,

I would recite the old story from memory.
Its diction had nursed me

at my bedside. Mother taught me
how grandfather

stripped his children's backs
with a switch; how he held them

under water. Mother taught me
the old story

so that its nutrients might fortify
my blood. At the head

of the class, I tilted my neck
and spread my arms to speak it.

But I couldn't predict
how the words would turn fragile and molt

in fluorescent classroom light.
How the other children

would corner me later, and call me
the beast who bays in the night.

The Single Drop

I get the dreamer
in my nature
from my father
whom I've never
even seen. I wonder
whether he is also
just a dream—a cloud
of cream that leaked
from the trunk
of a black walnut tree
and got smeared
on my mother's jeans
as she leaned against it
in a rare moment
of inactivity; the worker bee
of her soul just needing
a nanosecond to stop
and breathe,
unknowingly exchanging
the crop
for the single drop
of waste
that would become me.

The Dovecote

Being first fertile, the eldest
covers the pigeons with dew. Scythes
rend the dovecote in two. Somebody plunders
the birds. A deacon at church
smooths her nametag flat
against her chest: a gnarled hand
caught on a brainiac's tiny bra strap.

We live in a time of darkness
that we architected. We lunge
for lavender, forgetting
that it's made of blue. Outside, the icicles
poniard downward, dumbly murdering.
The perfect weapon, they disappear.

Instructions for the Human

I.

First, the trees disliked me.
Then the woods expelled me.

Urgent, I spoke from a blank surface
and was carved a mouth.

As soon
as I wriggled my fingers to test

their strength, my wrist
was re-fastened.

A lonely artisan understood himself
to be my father. Only after his disappearance

did I long for instruction
and know to call that longing *love*.

II.

In the house of the man who made me,
the kitchen walls are dusted with drawings

in cheap chalks: blackberries, locusts, and eggs. I jam
a knuckle into the plaster each time

the cut inside me
reopens. I learn

to call the cut *hunger*; learn to lunge
for the last scrap.

III.

I was forbidden from the audience,
and forbidden from the stage.

But in that place
I had a name. The marionettes

called me into my body—called me
"little pine tree" to show me

how natural I am.
Then they were snatched into the blackness

behind the curtain.
I would never have friends.

In my throat
I felt the hole the word *absence* is attached to.

There was nowhere else to go but home.

IV.

The summer is endless; means *waiting*. The bees
try to teach sensation, but my skin won't chip

against their stings. Pain
is just a brief indication

that tells the body how to keep itself
from dying; I worry the lesson

is wasted on me. Even the ghost
on my shoulder can smell the rosebush

in my father's yard. My nose
inches toward competence. I learn

to call this *education*, this deliberate chiseling
toward the correct form.

V.

Instruction made my body
possible. If you had been rude,

you might have described me
as wooden; many did, and I kicked them,

leaving an archive of bruises
behind me. It's true, I didn't have much

of a personality. Mostly, I wanted
joy. I have come to learn that the word

for this unriddable canker is *desire*.
See, I'm no dummy. I realize

what this life means: built by another's hand,
you gradually come to understand the self

as someone else's inscription.
The mirror

has been no help
for so long now. If only

someone could tell me the word
for what I am.

The Puppet's Education

I run from the classroom
after the teacher asks us
to measure gravity. I never wanted

to go to school anyway; the lessons
seemed designed to modify me.
In the trees, I hear breath

behind me, and it's the same story:
I can never be totally sure what it is
that's hunting me.

I hide under the largest fern
by the path in the woods
and wait. In the distance,

I hear the coach. Its bells
chime like the silvery spittle of infants;
its wheels crunch the road like a fairy's flatulence.

Upon its approach, a plump man
in a burgundy suit descends its delicate,
groaning steps. His face is pink

against the deeper rose of the coach's interior—
a fabric so shiny it must be oiled meat.
His moustache is blond; I hadn't imagined

hair to come in yellow! He extends
his thick fist toward me, to where I crouch
between the fronds. I think he means

to grasp my hand and lift me,
make a parabola with my body, understanding
how I ache to be suspended,

as if by strings—to be perpetually dizzy,
dependent on air. But he just pulls me
into the coach and tosses me

onto the shiny red chair. I think of the lesson
we were taught in class. Assembled
at the window, we watched through the glass

as a kite ascended, then crashed, its flight aborted
as the wind died, in compliance with its nature.
Nothing can float forever, said the physics teacher.

Damage

When I broke the wet branch,
it made the muffled sound

of failure. I wonder if childhood ends
with the overpowering

of weaker life. I was always meant
to be a student

of physics—measuring weight
and gravity, calculating force. Predicting

how the rapture would unfold
on its way down.

Who would yield
in the first, wet second? Would we be haunted

by the sounds of our damage?
When the rapture came, I raised

my hand. Surrounding bones
broke softly in turn.

IV.

Osteology

"It is an elastic column, and must first bend
before it breaks. When fracture occurs, it is almost
invariably the result of direct violence."

—Henry Gray
Anatomy, Descriptive and Surgical (1858)

The Gloomy Festival of Punishment

Floodlit, the actors move their arms.
Their mouths close and reopen.

The baritone safely strokes
the brocade of his costume.

When we stand at the intermission,
our seats clack inward.

The lobby shimmers, restored
to the splendors of the railroad age.

The tuxedos bandy at the concession:
"Wine!"—"Tea!"—"Wine!"

The early meal shifts in our stomachs, and nobody knows how
much money we make.

The women move their arms, and their mouths
close and reopen

as they lotion their elbows
with pomegranate extract.

Their necks, accoutered in open oyster shells,
grimly signify viscera.

Ushers hawk cheeses and cured meats
dotted with fat.

The children are strict,
choosing crudités over creampuffs,

licking bits of paper napkin
from wet ribs of celery.

Someone stabs a pickpocket's hand
with a broken champagne flute.

When the chimes direct us
back into the theatre, we unfold

our seats in a practiced gesture. Our hands
graze the green velour.

We peer at the proscenium
through the murky light, muttering *oh!* and *ah!*

and impatiently rustling. At the performance's conclusion,
we dutifully stand.

To produce the sound of applause, we criticize
our wrists into welts

with the wooden blades of our fans.
It must look accidental

when we cut our fingertips
along the glistening edges of our programs.

Art History

Assailant sculptor,

deliver the shape
from inside the raw block.

As you patiently hammer,

each flake of bone
surrenders to your vision.

Though the critics cry butchery,

remember how you spent yourself
in the rhythm of the chisel

to expose the blue vein.

The Doll

As you choke me, I say over and over
I am a doll.

I imagine how my face whitens
in your grip.

Every morning, a dream
becomes a nightmare—a tooth

pulled from the root. I cry like an infant,
waking into open fields of fear.

I walk to the school and I walk
to the store, clattering and clacking,

making whatever sound
a hollow thing makes.

It's sunny outside,
and sometimes the lilacs have bloomed.

But I always go back.
Again and again, I open

the door of the apartment:
leaning from the waist,

extending and retracting
until my joints shine with wear.

Then we curl up
on the sofa together.

I ask you to tell me the story
of how a rock becomes

an agate. How sand
becomes glass. Tell me the story

of how the marionette
becomes a real girl.

There

In the darkness
of the tractor shed, the body
is barely visible, huddled

next to the implements
that furrow the flesh
of the field. The body

is left there
after the blades of the thresher
have done their terrible work.

In the darkness
of the tractor shed, the body
tries to insist on its existence.

Pain roosts in the joints,
threatening to become
matter. The slow cut

of the winter wind
penetrates through the cracks
in the building's frame.

In the darkness
of the tractor shed, nothing
has definition. There,

there is no fear, because
there is nothing
to fear. There, it's easy

to withdraw to death, because death
is so white; it has no definition. There,
there. A pulse is useless:

there is nothing left to beat.

An Art of Unbearable Sensations

I bought you a brocade jacket in Toulouse
and then unlaced you out of it

in your apartment's kitchen. You hewed
a snail's trail in my pant leg while the rack's

unopened wines filtered the afternoon sun
in an aubergine paisley against the white walls.

I thought of the little canoe
we accidentally tipped

into the freezing lake.
I thought of the silent black-and-white film

I made of you in the bathtub, lunging
over its rim, spitting out water.

Why couldn't I stay
in the hot-hearted place you made

when I laced my fingers together?
When we first met, you told me about the time

God directed you to put stones in your pocket
and wait for his instructions

at the bottom of a pond. How cruel I was
in my art, to have made you

pantomime drowning. I didn't become cold-blooded,
but realized I was already,

like a stone house in its first autumn loses its heat,
recognizing its constitution.

Almost Without Touching the Body

Though we are both animals, tiny fibers
of the helix loosen between us,
fraying into unknowable species.

Your vocal cords thrum properly,
but the word tangles: the caught bird
of a hurt language.

Settle close on my mouth
and let your breath resolve
the untranslatable bells

of the sentence.
In this difficult era of ruined verbs,
I wish you wouldn't try to speak.

Just bring on the strange noise,
and the awkward heat of the beak.

Introductory Anatomy;
or, Prayer for the Withheld Interior

Is that your soul, or documents
marked with stenography?

I never know if you are human
or only an elegant human theory; a surface

of undiscovered knowledge
upon which to practice my tools.

Stethoscope:
> (the whole winter within you swirls like the empty conch)

Speculum:
> (the pink sheen of delicate skins which once were invisible)

Scalpel:
> (just one lock of hair to press between the pages
> of *Memoirs of Hadrian*)

Appendix and Index:
> (what do you mean when you say, "The era
> of you and me is over," and on which pages inside you
> might I find the word "over"?)

Trojan Horse

Never doubt
that you are beautiful.
But the wind

still blows
through the fields, bending
the stalks of wheat.

Never doubt
that when I invited you in,
I assented.

I didn't believe in peace;
never. I didn't believe
in surrender or flight.

I only longed to die
in blue robes
in your proximity.

Never doubt the memory
of my legs stiff
against yours in lovemaking. Never

wonder if you will wither
with the rest
of the skeletons. No matter;

my body has fallen
to you.
The sculpture

of your muscle
suits me; your proud murder
suits me. I am

like this; I am like this;
even in battle
I am like this: yours,

yours.
Leather and wood
against my blood.

V.

The Blood-Vascular System

"Wounds of the heart are often immediately fatal."

—Henry Gray
Anatomy, Descriptive and Surgical (1858)

Resident Taxonomist of the Great Lost and Found

Heaven was the hand
that finally managed to strike you back.

Angels appeared at your bedside,
robes dirty at the hems, emerging

from a wasteland of cumulus gases.
Mouths stinking of sulfur,

they clawed themselves ragged
fighting over your body.

They dragged you by the hamstring,
by the shoulder, and by the scruff, toppling

the stacks of books and papers
crowding the floor of your trailer.

I suspect you walk crooked now
in the afterlife. There, you catalogue

each shattered finger,
blackened eye, and bruised jaw—

all the bodies broken
by domestication. Their souls

have been processed for healing
but their carcasses remain,

littering the archive's
humid hallways. You tend to this detritus

like a scientist, each organ and appendage
suspended in mason jars

you filch from the kitchen staff.
Someday, when they retire you, the next taxonomist

will place your skin among the glass vessels, too.
It will curl up, embracing itself

like a baby. Like something
that hasn't been harmed yet.

Gatherers

One hunter put to bed.
One still haunting

the outermost edge
of the field at night.

There are so many reasons
we cannot retire the scythe.

Its possession
doesn't calm us—

we've already seen the deer
hugging the arrow.

We've carried our fear so long
it has dislocated our shoulders.

If we put the fear down,
there amongst the potatoes,

the soil won't aerate,
and all our meals will taste of it.

If we put the fear down,
we'll just gather it up again, laboring

during the harvest, turning
heavy from its starch. Better to carry it, then,

lest it become our only crop.

The Last Heirloom

When you died, an insect
crawled from the bathtub drain,

undrownable. Then my houseplant
withered, too. I refuse to remove it,

having come to identify soil
with death. I taste metal under my tongue

in tap water. I study only astrology,
Jung, and Buddhist texts, learning how

to fault myself
properly. Everything fails;

why must we patter so steadily after
redemption? You must have forgotten

how gently you pressed your heart to my ear
when I was a child,

because you labored in terror
against your last minutes, gripping

the fattened arms of your daughters, who still,
despite your cruelty, had not left you.

If I discover that I've inherited
the pale vegetable of your hatred,

I too might do as you have done.
I might hoard it. I might feed it.

I might nurture it
as my only achievement.

Then I might panic to feel it uprooted
and pulled from my throat.

The Pathologist's Notes

Finally, I can stare at you
without shame.

I predict the bones
of your clavicle will be wet

beneath the pale page
with which they are covered.

A hollow click:
your disobedient wrist.

Under the enterotome's
weird blade,

the bruises
corrode inside you.

They chart a black stain
up the length of your spine.

One summer, you told me
your favorite word,

just as a bluebird
thudded against the window.

Your smallest organs disentangle
under the tutelage

of my fists. Still, the needle
is difficult to thread.

Do you resist
science?

Embalmer's Oath

Camphor
helps the heartsick

outlast us. Marrowless,
after the throat

sung bone. The medicine
haunts us, healing only

in the invisible register.
Healing only

the girl without hands.
Lancet and ash

haggle the wrist. Snow
makes the heart sing

bone. Who
would have asked

for this career: snow
and camphor?

The medicine heals
only the dead. Who

could've predicted our
wax-jointed victory?

Aftershave

The hangman leaves work
with hemp fibers clinging to his coat.
The rope burn edged into his palm
reopens at home
as he lifts the whistling kettle
from the stove. He can't shake
the scent of aftershave. Of all the last gestures,
that one haunts him the most.
He wonders if the smell—
so similar to his grandmother's
chokecherry tincture—
had transferred to his hands
as they looped the noose
around the inmate's throat.

The Miser

After so much violence, every gift
was an organ donation. Each time
I had to ask myself if I could function
without such a crucial possession. My blood
became sluggish with fear
of how the loss would feel the moment
I handed over the favor, the compliment,
or the cup of sugar. Shaking, I'd spill
the grains to the floor or garble
the gesture in some other way, saving
the recipient from taking on this dead heart
no preventative medicine could ever warm
into natural throbbing.
What is the lesson about surrender
I was put here to learn?

VI.

The Lymphatics

"When the fragments are cleared away,
the orbit will be exposed."

—Henry Gray
Anatomy, Descriptive and Surgical (1858)

The Magician, Reversed

You thought the prairie
had settled. You thought
the corn yellow.

You thought the bees.

But look forward
into the day: the sun will rise
from whichever direction

you ask me to call it.

I wish you could have seen me
ride the grey horse
through the pasture like a hearse,

dividing the grasses.

I wish you could have seen the foxglove
genuflect and wither,
or the grains capitulate.

I wish you could have seen

the tender seedpods
confess their viscera.
The new world is lush

with what I cause.

Even the sky
cleaves and releases its blue
at the warning of my hand.

Declensions from the Infinitive

The apartments had been a sanctuary
against the disappointments
of existence. But autumn came
and, in its splendor, was relentless.

The tenants were inspired
to open their windows. They deemed the season
exact in its description; no elaborate conjugation,
only a lonely ochre leaf.

They stretched over their windowsills
toward the boulevard, for the dying
maple. The leaf, flaming, detached
in answer. A young boy in a baseball cap

leaned his tiny body forward
and lunged to grasp it. But he had failed
to understand physics. When he fell
from the top-floor apartment, it was right.

The Ancient Dream of the Evolutionist

At night the winter breeds ice,
white as fresh paper.

Every morning
I sketch the edges
of the recurring nightmare:

the pale, cowering boy
whose spine secretes blood.

In my clumsiness, ink
forever pools
from the blotter onto the desk.

I press the ink into the grain, and resist
just before tasting it.

The black stains on my fingertips
lengthen toward my wrists,
like colonists.

In the howling whiteness,
the draft from the open flue

wrestles the fire. The pale ghost
maintains an invisible fist
against the snow's crust. He disappears

each time I depict him, refusing
compliance. Perhaps there had been

a relation between us,
but he has unloosened it,
despite the ancient dream of the evolutionist.

No science can scrub the ink
as it travels my arms.

The Tasks of the Dwelling

In the cruelest days, the temperature
was twenty below zero.

Through the window, I saw that the snow
had built multiple layers

and was covered in ice.
The tires of my car

had deflated sometime in the night. A squirrel
had frozen to the hood.

I felt safe in my woolen socks,
sipping my steaming mug of spiced tea, curled

in my antique armchair, flipping
a book's pages. I didn't notice

when the door handle
frosted over. I couldn't pinpoint

the moment I started to see my breath.
All I knew

was that I couldn't allow the pipes
to freeze. There was nothing to do

but apply myself to the tasks
of the dwelling. I turned on

the hair dryer and the clothes dryer. I turned on
the iron; I breathed on the glass.

I opened the taps, and bid
the most scalding water forward.

The pipes clicked and shuddered
as though they had shoulders;

they whined, like the squirrel
in his antepenultimate moments.

At the cough of the kitchen faucet,
I came with a bucket.

Then the bath bloodlet its rust,
and all the plumbing responded

in counterpoint, its open-throated warble
softening the floorboards.

I felt sick, but of course
the toilet was unusable now.

The External World of Impermanent Phenomena

Past the naked mannequin in the window,
I see my lover at the register, shrouding
a pair of socks in tissue paper
and placing them in a glossy bag.
I take off my mittens and press my palms
to the window, as though touching the glass
will close the distance. Behind me,
the homeless ukulele player
warbles a ballad of love and blunts
the strings of his instrument with a curled fist.

Forecast

Cranes
arrive from the east.
We put on our cleats
and circle the marsh
to puncture their nests. Unless
they are forced, they stay
the winter, their delicate legs
frozen in mud,
like hieroglyphs
predicting our bleak future.

Petals
of withering lilacs
float to the sidewalk.
They're gathered by children
who glue them to paper
in accidental configurations.

The cars
in our small city
make tight turns.
They intuit
merges and execute
only necessary motions. Few
flourishes. They navigate
o and u and misspell
obfuscation. Their visible breaths
betray them.

The knitters
stitch their fingers together
with nettles, forcing
prayer. The drama of their clothing
is small; smaller.

Only the cabaret performers
disobey the weather.

They pass the season
in leotards and shiny tights,
smoking behind the derelict theater,
blowing shapeless clouds
into the overcast sky.
Showing us what we lose
when we try to make sense.

Lessons in Physics

Nobody told us
we would grow old
inside small houses;

our rectangle gardens
hitched to the backs of our garages,
with three weak tomatoes
considering red.

We couldn't predict
how everything would obey
small rules; how
their smallness
would capture us, making us

nearly invisible;
all our movements
completed inside a circle,
a track trod
until it furrows:
bedroom, kitchen, bathroom, bedroom.

We walk a careful path
between objects: less touching
the difficult surfaces; less
brushing against the stucco
or smelling the papery rot

of the birches; less
pushing our limits to friction
until we no longer snap
into flame, never crack

with energy. How life
succumbs to half-life.
How the body wants entropy.

The Old Property

At the old property, dragonfly larvae
skim the pond. The asters
bend in lassitude.
Little blunders

ask nothing of us,
escaping unregistered. Blood
corrodes the tractor chains
in the shed.

The house gives us dreams now.
Under the eaves
roost the cataracts—
artifacts from the lost years.

The pinecones in our shoes:
a penance. The violets creep the grounds
like mold,
like grief.

The Split Fig

When we tired of stained glass,
we manufactured halogen.

It was holy
because it shined.

But its chemistry would not heat, despite
how we breathed with devotion,

our mouths hovering over the bulbs,
transferring energy

in a warm fog. We could not understand
what we had done wrong.

In penance
we fastened our eyelids

with a hot glue gun, choosing
unknowing. We pinched

our noses with clothespins,
and the smell of the split fig

rotting at the tree's roots
could no longer

admonish us. Like this, we discovered
anesthesia. This

was the lesson of science:
our suffering

turned out to have
some permanent use.

Past Civilization

All day the corpses pile up,
lining the sidewalks.
At night the dump trucks come.

The gods can hear our bones crack
in the compactors.

The machines are so burdened
that they regularly need
to be repaired, their technicians attuned

to the moment our bodies become
unbearable.

The streets are swept in the blackest hours
so the children can awake
into a recurring emptiness:

an unsoiled place
where nothing happened the day before.

We don't even leave
ghosts behind anymore.
All we have left is the single secret

we whisper furtively amongst each other
before the next person disappears:

past civilization, past
the boxwood hedges, past the homesteads
and the sunflower fields, beyond

the wild plains with their yellowing
heather, there is the gaping,

aching ground
in which they dispose of us. Only there
can we finally be safe together.

End of Days

Fire whitens
on the driveway, melting
the handles of the old bicycle.
We'll have to replace them

with wings; the curved back
of the beetle its seat; the legs
of the grasshopper—extracted
from a bead of amber
found in a museum's ashes—
its new spinal frame.

In a project like this,
it's best to use materials
you will never have to strip—
it's bad luck to contradict
the natural grain.

In this new world, human joints
are old-fashioned, sketched
in anatomical drawings
with a patina that blooms

outward from the socket. Rust-colored,
fat and cartilage flake from hollow pockets.

Aesthetes' Manifesto

We will wear cloaks of silk
and bracelets of agates.
We'll hang tapestries

over the casement windows—
in lamplight their gold threads
will overshine the dull heat of the sun.

We will not remember our old lives:
how we circled bins of produce,
dialed disconnected numbers, and tried not to hope

for personal mail. How we scowled back
at the sidewalk that tripped us, to shift
the burden of shame.

In a white room at the world's edge, untouched
by persecution, we will watch
as the paintings age, as dust

settles into the cracks of the oil.
We'll perfume our wrists with myrrh
and practice complex elocution. Our organs

will turn to paper, ensuring
they never spoil.
This will be our new constitution.

VII.

The Organs of Special Sense

"The purified blood is carried back."

—Henry Gray
Anatomy, Descriptive and Surgical (1858)

The Organ Tuner

Thank you, mercury heart,
for your accurate measure
of barometric pressure

and imperfect temperature.
Winds lean from the east
and stir fine hairs at the follicle,

but you are infallible.
I trust you to counterstrike
when the hunter nuzzles under

my skirt. Otherwise, I won't
be able to cool.
When I'm offered daffodils,

candies, and love notes
written on scraps of graph paper,
I trust you will teach me

how to be cruel.
When I hear a holler
across the water and discover

that someone is drowning,
I trust you to turn me away
from the pool.

Ecology 101

Like an animal, I understand
the boundaries of my habitat.
I eat the bounty and circumvent
the poisonous plants. I ride
what offers itself to be ridden.
I can catch the scent of a predator's sweat
on the shifting wind.

When I hear the architect coming
over the plain, his T-square and protractor
clicking against his hip, I hide
in the cattails. He means to measure
the acres and pave them over.
He means to lure all the species together
and light the meadow on fire.

But I can pick the cherries from his trap
without it snapping.

The Skeleton Builder

The doctor says
>> bones become stronger

>> the longer a person carries
>> a heavy load. He's referring to fat,

>> but that's not the weightiest burden
>> the body bears. That, perhaps,

>> would be an overstuffed backpack.
>> Or maybe the liver, besotted with love.

>>> Sadness, that onerous mass,
>> feels even closer

>> to the truth. But it's too light—
>> too brief—too impermanent—

>> to be of use. At one shade removed,
>> the body's stubbornest bruise must surely be

grief, that rotten petunia.

Grief, the teabag heart
>> that flavors the blood.

Grief the coagulant, persuading your blood
>> to stop running, turning
>> itself to tar.

Grief, the castor oil
>> that tightens intestines, making us
>> clean.

Grief the surgeon,
>> erasing the person.

Grief, the brutal historian
        in the bowels
        of the building, combing
        the record for the tiniest facts.
        Committing the most excruciating ones
        to memory.

Grief, the moss
        you stumble upon in the deepest part
        of the forest. It covers the boulders
        and creeps up the trees.
        It's so tender
        and fluorescent. Probably because
        everything around it
        is so dark.

Grief, the fetters
        that chain your convict ankles together,
        binding the parts of your body that otherwise
        would've defected by now. It's the part of you
        that people hear coming—the irons clanking
        and the ball thudding against the floor
        as you shuffle and shrug down the hallways, always
        relearning to walk.

Grief, that labor pain, bringing
        something into the world
        you are obligated to love.
        The quiet bundle
        strapped to your back,
        shaping your muscles.
        The good baby:
        the one who never cries.

Grief, the skeleton builder,
        forging a structure
        immune to fracture.

Grief—not the winter
        but the evergreen. Persistent,
        it will thrive
        after everything around it dies.

Ah, grief. The particles of dust
        that are always in the air,
        but that only
        a certain slant of light
        makes visible.

It Is No Longer the Body,
with the Ritual Play of Excessive Pains

I am done with machines
and enter the natural world.

There is nothing
to hold me here, at the edge of the water,

       where salt eats the skin off this cage.

          The harsh wind
          exposes the fractured skeleton,

leaching its marrow, unbinding its joints.

The rusted gears of the heart
      catch and crumble.
      I ask you to
      burgle their chambers
          and place the old name that you called me by

      on the architect's table.
      It will be laid to rest
      with other useless tools

of measurement. Only sand understands me now:
      individual grains beaten smaller and smaller.

The old name that you called me by

flattens. It skips twice against the water
and sinks.

The Haunted Book

Tell me what you find
in the distance. Shape the distance

correctly, so I can
inhabit its contours

unabridged, in the original
Latin, untouched

by translation.
Each generation

has been assigned its lesson
to break the spine. Its ink

has been culled
from the blood of our ghosts.

Composed in iambics, it sutures
the heartbeat

to the hand. By the time
you open it, you will have

spoken it in the future imperative,
irregular and defective; your body

patterned after its reference;
burnished and burnished until

you have become as unmodified
as the first noun.

It is your turn
to pass the book down.

Notes

The following poem titles are lines quoted from Michel Foucault's *Discipline and Punish*:

"The Punishments Must Be a School"
"An Art of Unbearable Sensations"
"Almost Without Touching the Body"
"The Gloomy Festival of Punishment"
"Resident Taxonomist of the Great Lost and Found"
"The External World of Impermanent Phenomena"
"It Is No Longer the Body, with the Ritual Play of Excessive Pains"

About the Author

Emily August is an Associate Professor of Literature at Stockton University. Nominated for a Pushcart Prize and Best New Poets, her poems have appeared in *Callaloo*, *Cimarron Review*, *Ninth Letter*, *Southern Humanities Review*, and elsewhere. She divides her time between Lake Superior's North Shore and the Atlantic Ocean's Jersey Shore.

About the Artist

Born and raised in the upper Midwest, Shawna Gilmore commonly uses vintage photos, patterns, and interior/exterior elements in her surreal paintings. She graduated in 2000 from the University of Minnesota-Duluth with a BFA in Studio Art, Emphasis on Drawing and Printmaking. Her winter-forged imagination generates character-driven, narrative paintings that explore chameleonic behaviors. https://www.shawnagilmore.com

About The Word Works

Since its founding in 1974, The Word Works has steadily published volumes of contemporary poetry and presented public programs. Its imprints include The Washington Prize, The Tenth Gate Prize, The Hilary Tham Capital Collection, and International Editions.

Monthly, The Word Works offers free programs in its Café Muse Literary Salon. Starting in 2023, the winners of the Jacklyn Potter Young Poets Competition will be presented in the June Café Muse program.

As a 501(c)3 organization, The Word Works has received awards from the National Endowment for the Arts, the National Endowment for the Humanities, the D.C. Commission on the Arts & Humanities, the Witter Bynner Foundation, Poets & Writers, The Writer's Center, Bell Atlantic, the David G. Taft Foundation, and others, including many generous private patrons.

An archive of artistic and administrative materials in the Washington Writing Archive is housed in the George Washington University Gelman Library. The Word Works is a member of the Community of Literary Magazines and Presses and its books are distributed by Small Press Distribution.

wordworksbooks.org

Other Word Works Books

Annik Adey-Babinski, *Okay Cool No Smoking Love Pony*
Karren L. Alenier, *From the Belly: Poets Respond to Gerturude Stein's Tender Buttons*
Karren L. Alenier, *Wandering on the Outside*
Jennifer Barber, *The Sliding Boat Our Bodies Made*
Andrea Carter Brown, *September 12*
Willa Carroll, *Nerve Chorus*
Grace Cavalieri, *Creature Comforts / The Long Game: Poems Selected & New*
Abby Chew, *A Bear Approaches from the Sky*
Nadia Colburn, *The High Shelf*
Henry Crawford, *The Binary Planet*
Barbara Goldberg, *Berta Broadfoot and Pepin the Short / Breaking & Entering: New and Selected Poems*
Akua Lezli Hope, *Them Gone*
Michael Klein, *The Early Minutes of Without: Poems Selected & New*
Deborah Kuan, *Women on the Moon*
Frannie Lindsay, *If Mercy*
Elaine Magarrell, *The Madness of Chefs*
Chloe Martinez, *Ten Thousand Selves*
Marilyn McCabe, *Glass Factory*
JoAnne McFarland, *Identifying the Body*
Leslie McGrath, *Feminists Are Passing from Our Lives*
Kevin McLellan, *Ornitheology*
Ron Mohring, *The Boy Who Reads in the Trees*
A. Molotkov, *Future Symptoms*
Ann Pelletier, *Letter That Never*
W.T. Pfefferle, *My Coolest Shirt*
Ayaz Pirani, *Happy You Are Here*
Robert Sargent, *Aspects of a Southern Story / A Woman from Memphis*
Roger Smith, *Radiation Machine Gun Funk*
Jeddie Sophonius, *Love & Sambal*
Julia Story, *Spinster for Hire*
Leah Umansky, *Of Tyrant*
Barbara Ungar, *Naming the Animals*
Cheryl Clark Vermeulen, *They Can Take It Out*
Julie Marie Wade, *Skirted*
Miles Waggener, *Superstition Freeway*
Fritz Ward, *Tsunami Diorama*
Camille-Yvette Welsch, *The Four Ugliest Children in Christendom*
Amber West, *Hen & God*
Maceo Whitaker, *Narco Farm*

Printed in the USA
CPSIA information can be obtained
at www.ICGtesting.com
LVHW040426130824
788023LV00012B/767